copyright © 2020

All rights reserved.
No part of this publication
may be reproduced,
stored in a retrieval system,
or transmitted, in any form or
by any means, electronic,
mechanical, photocopying,
recording, or otherwise,
without the prior written
permission of the publisher.
Except in the case of brief
quotations embedded in
critical articles and reviews

Fashion
COLORING BOOK
For Girls

This BOOK Belongs to:

Merry Christmas

Printed in Great Britain
by Amazon